AF888400

THIS NOTEBOOK BELONGS TO

ISBN:978-1-958297-40-7

Corzo Creations, LLC

TO DO

Date:

Today's Focus

Priorities List

My Reminder

Notes

TO DO

Date:

Today's Focus

Priorities List

My Reminder

Notes

TO DO

Date:

Today's Focus

Priorities List

My Reminder

Notes

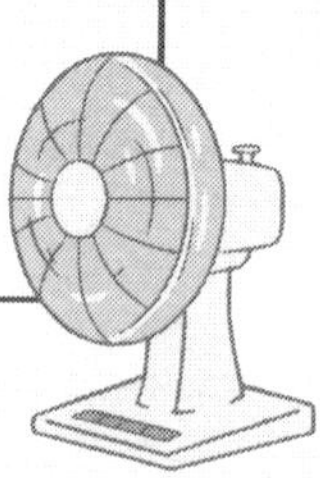

TO DO

Date:

Today's Focus

Priorities List

-
-
-
-
-
-
-
-
-

My Reminder

Notes

TO DO

Date:

Today's Focus

Priorities List

-
-
-
-
-
-
-
-
-

My Reminder

Notes

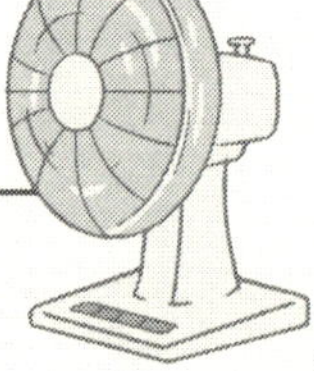

TO DO

Date:

Today's Focus

Priorities List

-
-
-
-
-
-
-
-
-

My Reminder

Notes

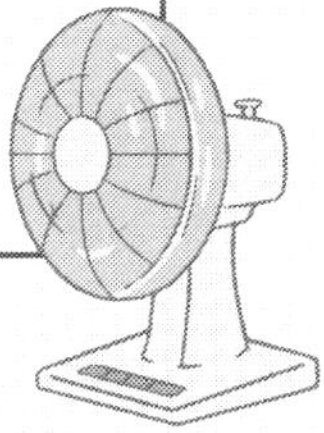

TO DO

Date:

Today's Focus

Priorities List

-
-
-
-
-
-
-
-
-

My Reminder

Notes

TO DO

Date:

Today's Focus

Priorities List

-
-
-
-
-
-
-
-
-

My Reminder

Notes

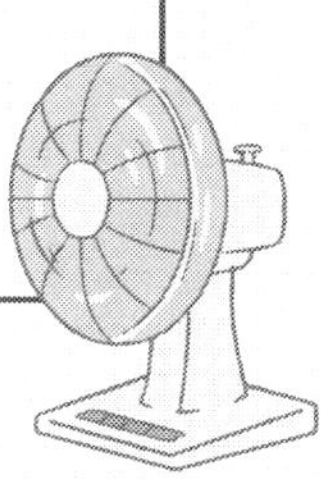

TO DO

Date:

Today's Focus

Priorities List

-
-
-
-
-
-
-
-
-

My Reminder

Notes

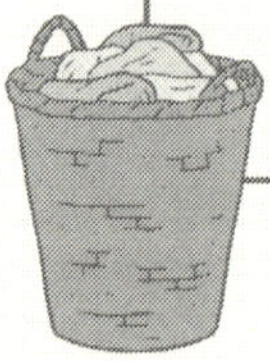

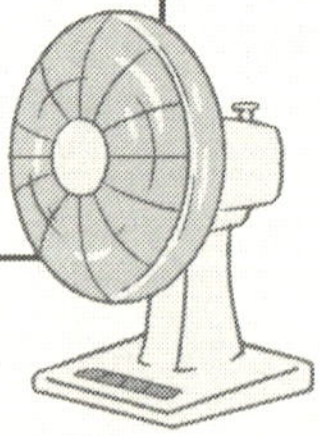

TO DO

Date:

Today's Focus

Priorities List

-
-
-
-
-
-
-
-
-

My Reminder

Notes

TO DO

Date:

Today's Focus

Priorities List

-
-
-
-
-
-
-
-
-

My Reminder

Notes

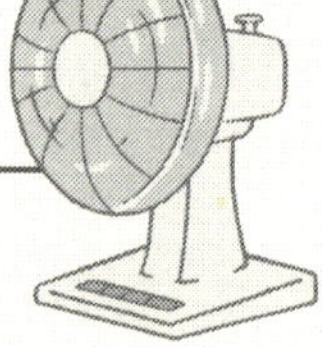

TO DO

Date:

Today's Focus

Priorities List

My Reminder

Notes

TO DO

Date:

Today's Focus

Priorities List

My Reminder

Notes

TO DO

Date:

Today's Focus

Priorities List

My Reminder

Notes

TO DO

Date:

Today's Focus

Priorities List

-
-
-
-
-
-
-
-
-

My Reminder

Notes

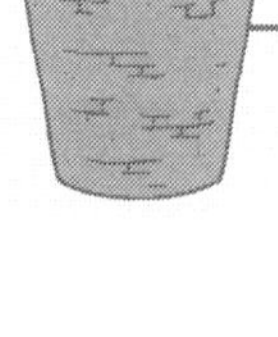

TO DO

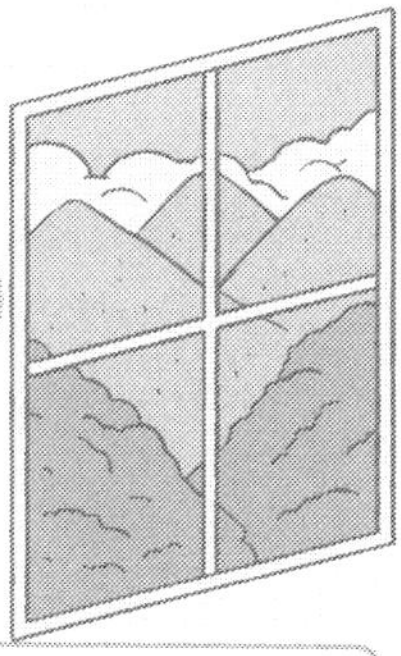

Date:

Today's Focus

Priorities List

My Reminder

Notes

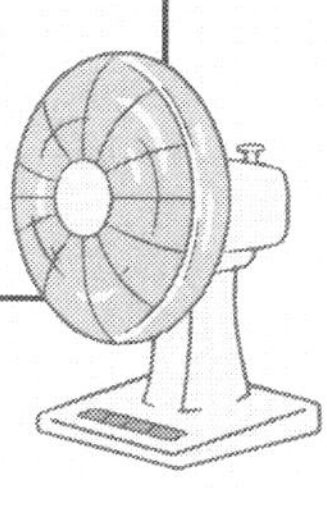

TO DO

Date:

Today's Focus

Priorities List

My Reminder

Notes

TO DO

Date:

Today's Focus

Priorities List

My Reminder

Notes

TO DO

Date:

Today's Focus

Priorities List

My Reminder

Notes

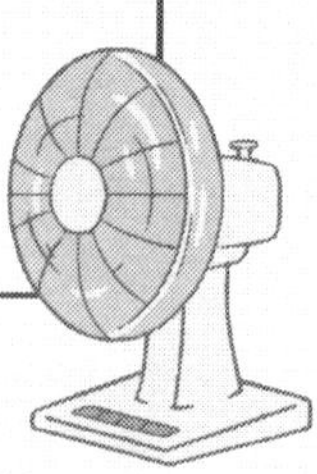

TO DO

Date:

Today's Focus

Priorities List

-
-
-
-
-
-
-
-
-

My Reminder

Notes

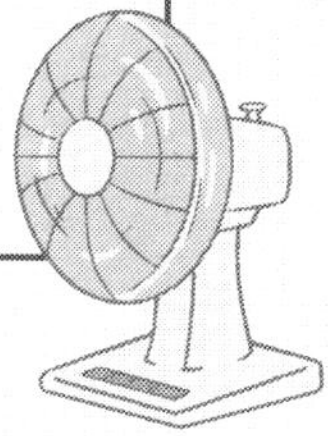

TO DO

Date:

Today's Focus

Priorities List

My Reminder

Notes

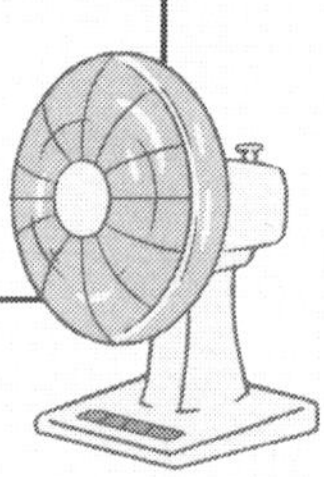

TO DO

Date:

Today's Focus

Priorities List

-
-
-
-
-
-
-
-
-

My Reminder

Notes

TO DO

Date:

Today's Focus

Priorities List

-
-
-
-
-
-
-
-
-

My Reminder

Notes

TO DO

Date:

Today's Focus

Priorities List

-
-
-
-
-
-
-
-
-

My Reminder

Notes

TO DO

Date:

Today's Focus

Priorities List

-
-
-
-
-
-
-
-
-

My Reminder

Notes

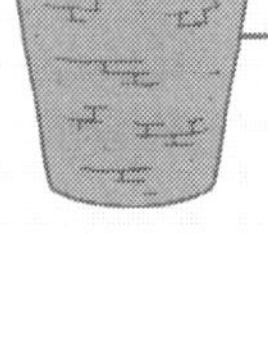

TO DO

Date:

Today's Focus

Priorities List

-
-
-
-
-
-
-
-
-

My Reminder

Notes

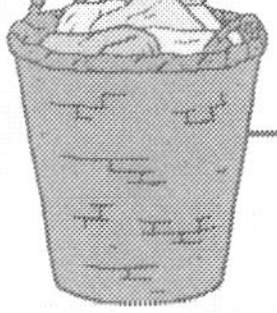

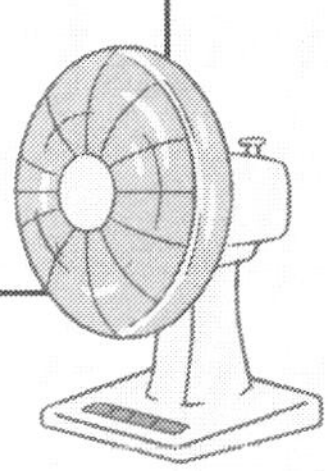

TO DO

Date:

Today's Focus

Priorities List

-
-
-
-
-
-
-
-
-

My Reminder

Notes

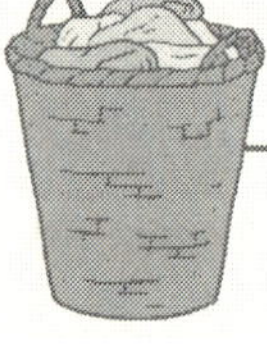

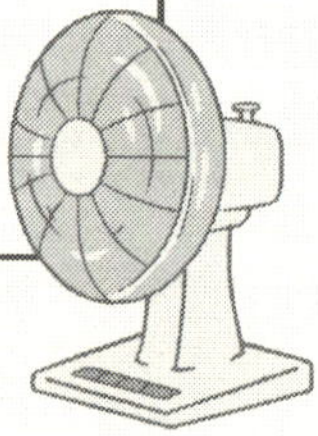

TO DO

Date:

Today's Focus

Priorities List

-
-
-
-
-
-
-
-
-

My Reminder

Notes

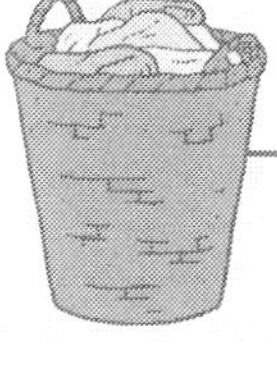

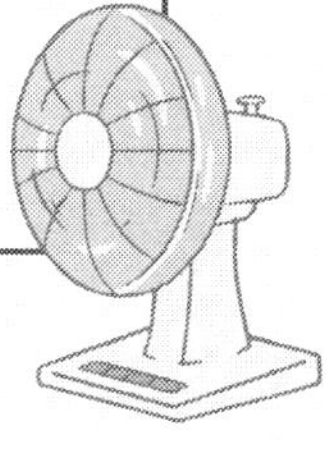

TO DO

Date:

Today's Focus

Priorities List

-
-
-
-
-
-
-
-
-

My Reminder

Notes

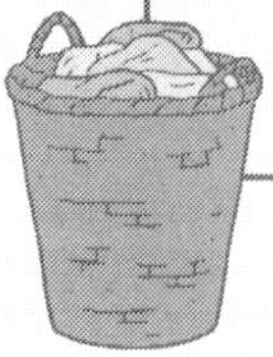

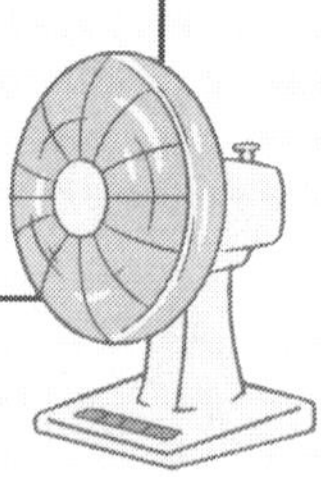

TO DO

Date:

Today's Focus

Priorities List

-
-
-
-
-
-
-
-
-

My Reminder

Notes

TO DO

Date:

Today's Focus

Priorities List

-
-
-
-
-
-
-
-
-

My Reminder

Notes

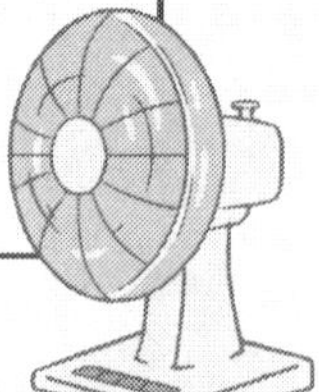

TO DO

Date:

Today's Focus

Priorities List

-
-
-
-
-
-
-
-
-

My Reminder

Notes

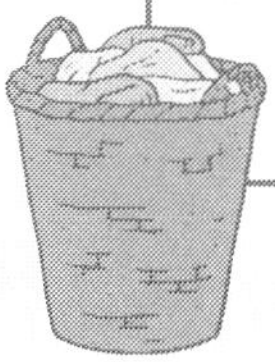

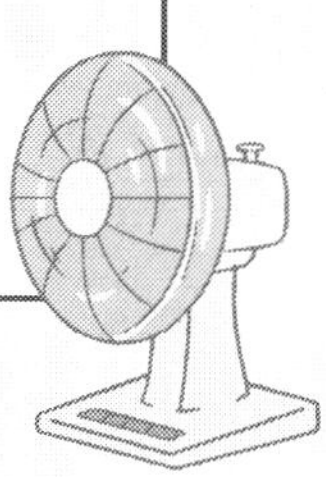

TO DO

Date:

Today's Focus

Priorities List

My Reminder

Notes

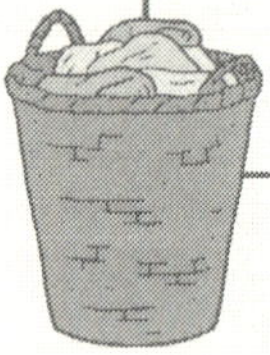

TO DO

Date:

Today's Focus

Priorities List

-
-
-
-
-
-
-
-
-

My Reminder

Notes

TO DO

Date:

Today's Focus

Priorities List

-
-
-
-
-
-
-
-
-

My Reminder

Notes

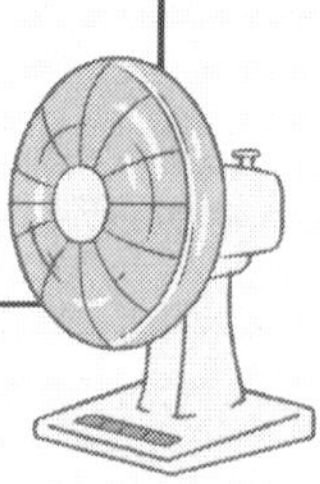

TO DO

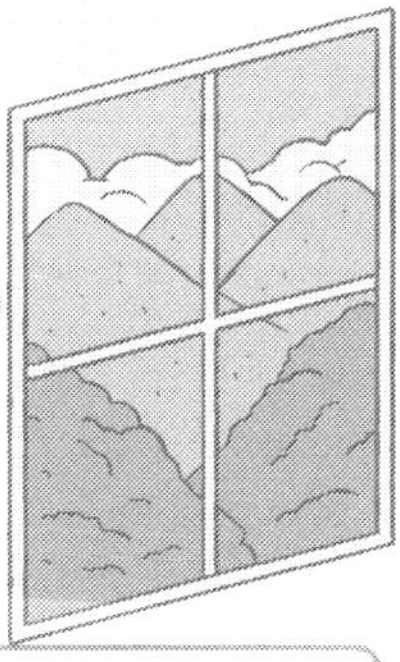

Date:

Today's Focus

Priorities List

-
-
-
-
-
-
-
-
-

My Reminder

Notes

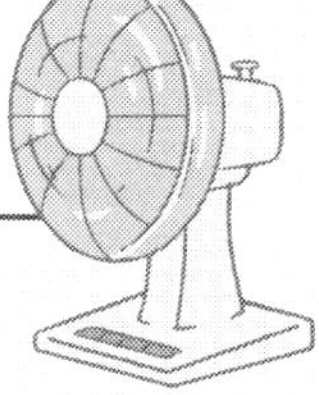

TO DO

Date:

Today's Focus

Priorities List

My Reminder

Notes

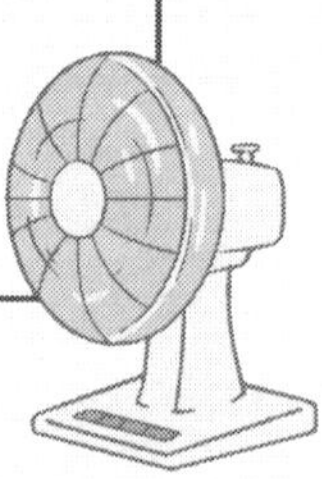

TO DO

Date:

Today's Focus

Priorities List

-
-
-
-
-
-
-
-
-

My Reminder

Notes

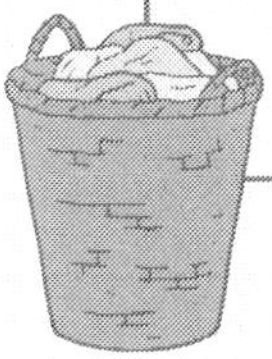

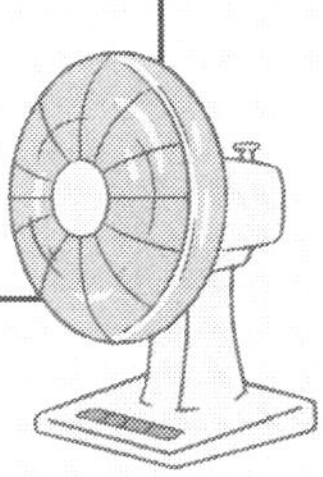

TO DO

Date:

Today's Focus

Priorities List

-
-
-
-
-
-
-
-
-

My Reminder

Notes

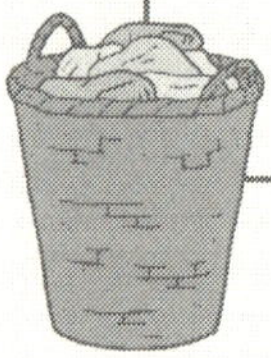

TO DO

Date:

Today's Focus

Priorities List

My Reminder

Notes

TO DO

Date:

Today's Focus

Priorities List

My Reminder

Notes

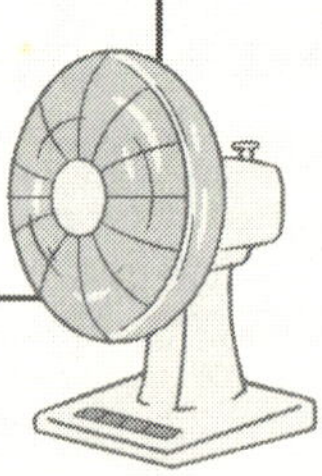

TO DO

Date:

Today's Focus

Priorities List

-
-
-
-
-
-
-
-
-

My Reminder

Notes

TO DO

Date:

Today's Focus

Priorities List

-
-
-
-
-
-
-
-
-

My Reminder

Notes

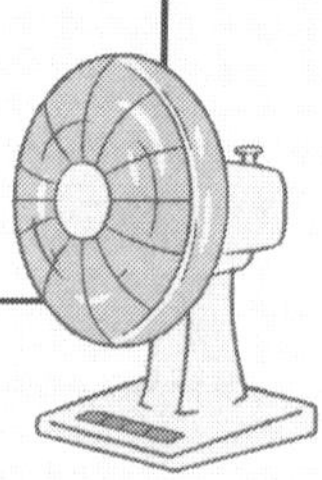

TO DO

Date:

Today's Focus

Priorities List

My Reminder

Notes

TO DO

Date:

Today's Focus

Priorities List

My Reminder

Notes

TO DO

Date:

Today's Focus

Priorities List

-
-
-
-
-
-
-
-
-

My Reminder

Notes

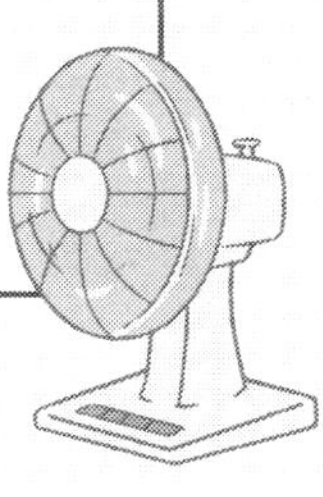

TO DO

Date:

Today's Focus

Priorities List

-
-
-
-
-
-
-
-
-

My Reminder

Notes

TO DO

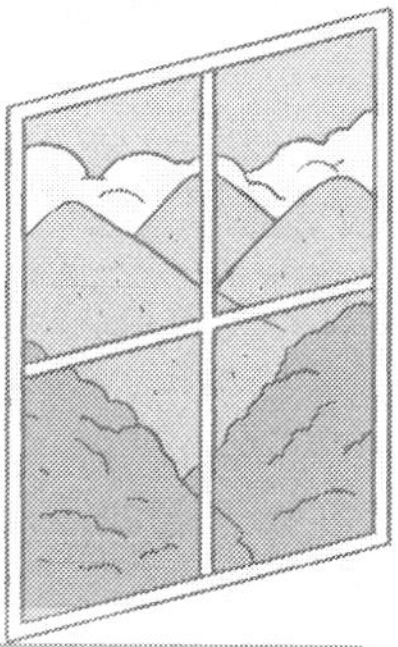

Date:

Today's Focus

Priorities List

-
-
-
-
-
-
-
-
-

My Reminder

Notes

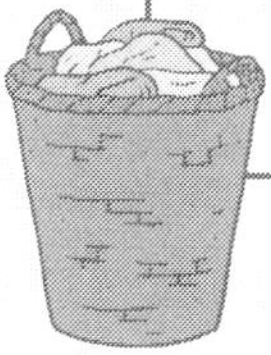

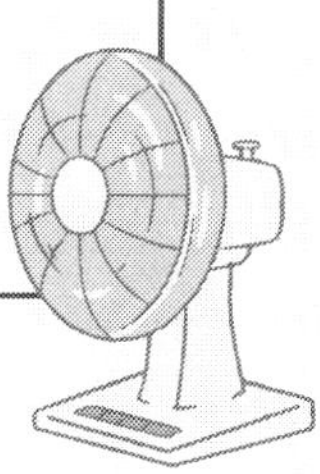

TO DO

Date:

Today's Focus

Priorities List

My Reminder

Notes

TO DO

Date:

Today's Focus

Priorities List

-
-
-
-
-
-
-
-
-

My Reminder

Notes

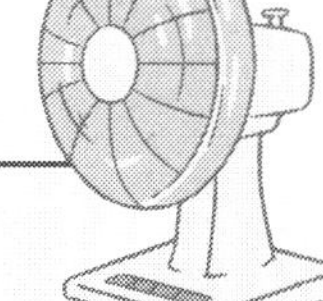

TO DO

Date:

Today's Focus

Priorities List

-
-
-
-
-
-
-
-
-

My Reminder

Notes

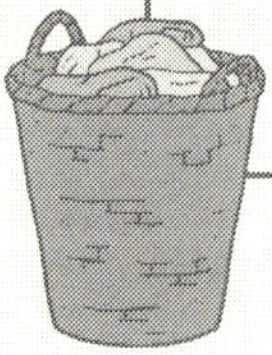

TO DO

Date:

Today's Focus

Priorities List

My Reminder

Notes

TO DO

Date:

Today's Focus

Priorities List

My Reminder

Notes

TO DO

Date:

Today's Focus

Priorities List

-
-
-
-
-
-
-
-
-

My Reminder

Notes

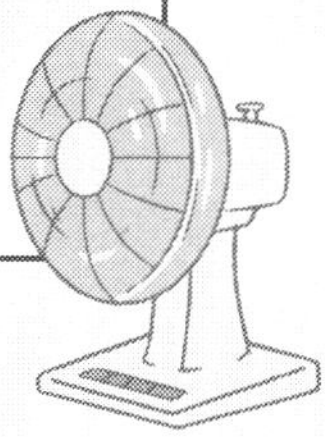

TO DO

Date:

Today's Focus

Priorities List

-
-
-
-
-
-
-
-
-

My Reminder

Notes

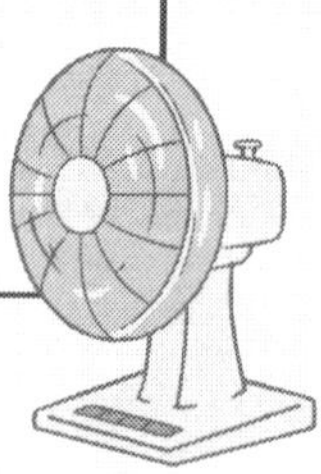

TO DO

Date:

Today's Focus

Priorities List

My Reminder

Notes

TO DO

Date:

Today's Focus

Priorities List

-
-
-
-
-
-
-
-
-

My Reminder

Notes

TO DO

Date:

Today's Focus

Priorities List

My Reminder

Notes

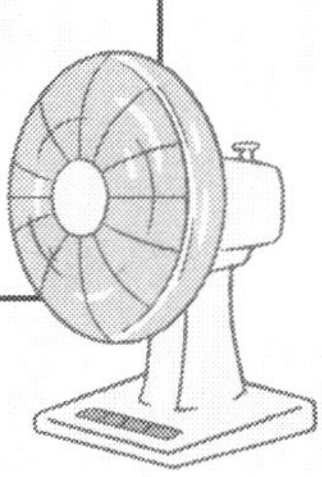

TO DO

Date:

Today's Focus

Priorities List

-
-
-
-
-
-
-
-
-

My Reminder

Notes

TO DO

Date:

Today's Focus

Priorities List

-
-
-
-
-
-
-
-
-

My Reminder

Notes

TO DO

Date:

Today's Focus

Priorities List

My Reminder

Notes

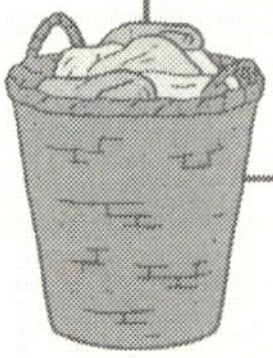

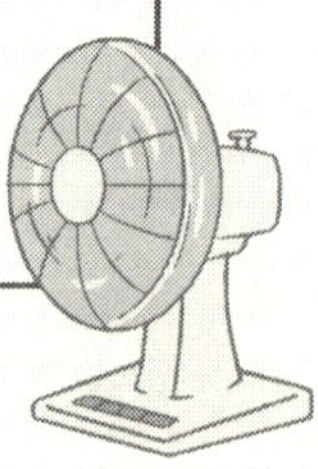

TO DO

Date:

Today's Focus

Priorities List

-
-
-
-
-
-
-
-
-

My Reminder

Notes

TO DO

Date:

Today's Focus

Priorities List

-
-
-
-
-
-
-
-
-

My Reminder

Notes

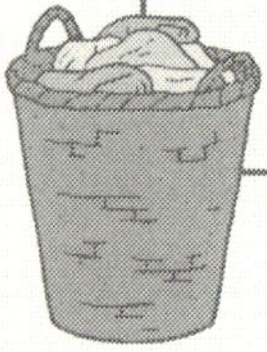

TO DO

Date:

Today's Focus

Priorities List

-
-
-
-
-
-
-
-
-

My Reminder

Notes

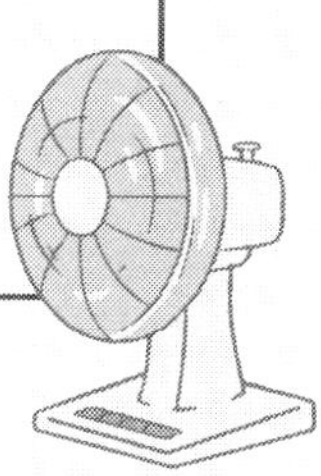

TO DO

Date:

Today's Focus

Priorities List

-
-
-
-
-
-
-
-
-

My Reminder

Notes

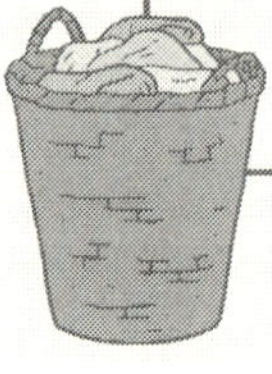

TO DO

Date:

Today's Focus

Priorities List

My Reminder

Notes

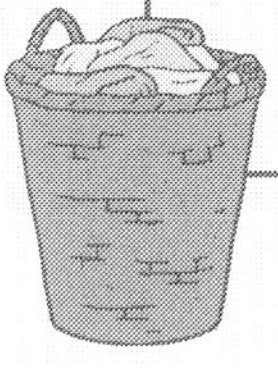

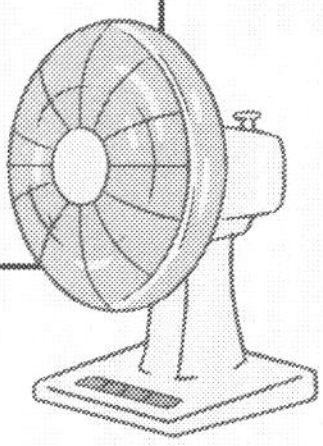

TO DO

Date:

Today's Focus

Priorities List

My Reminder

Notes

TO DO

Date:

Today's Focus

Priorities List

My Reminder

Notes

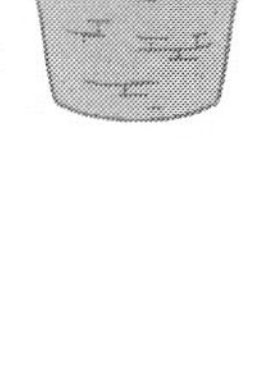

TO DO

Date:

Today's Focus

Priorities List

-
-
-
-
-
-
-
-
-

My Reminder

Notes

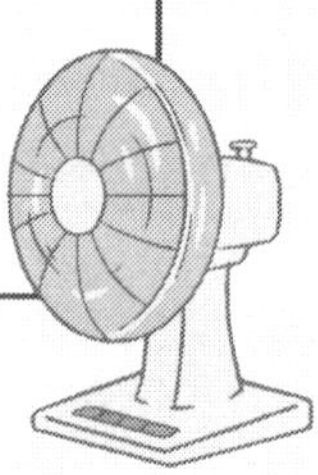

TO DO

Date:

Today's Focus

Priorities List

-
-
-
-
-
-
-
-
-

My Reminder

Notes

TO DO

Date:

Today's Focus

Priorities List

-
-
-
-
-
-
-
-
-

My Reminder

Notes

TO DO

Date:

Today's Focus

Priorities List

-
-
-
-
-
-
-
-
-

My Reminder

Notes

TO DO

Date:

Today's Focus

Priorities List

My Reminder

Notes

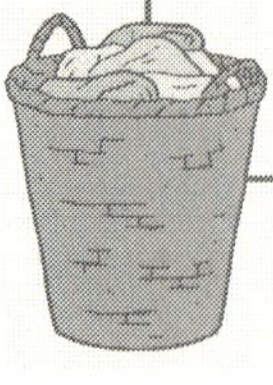

TO DO

Date:

Today's Focus

Priorities List

My Reminder

Notes

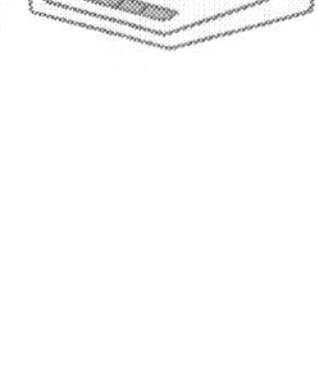

TO DO

Date:

Today's Focus

Priorities List

My Reminder

Notes

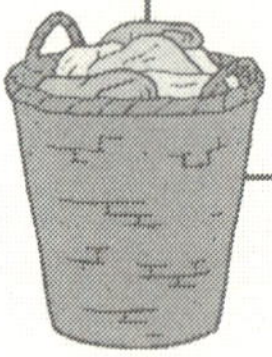

TO DO

Date:

Today's Focus

Priorities List

-
-
-
-
-
-
-
-
-

My Reminder

Notes

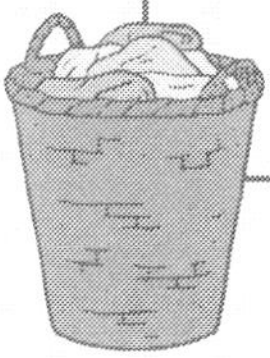

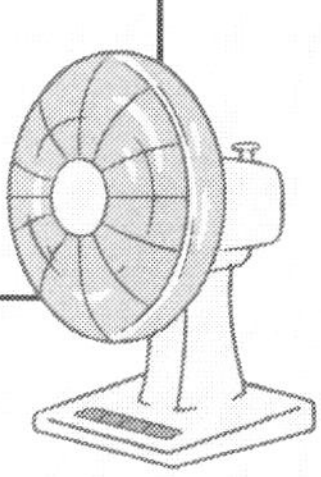

TO DO

Date:

Today's Focus

Priorities List

-
-
-
-
-
-
-
-
-

My Reminder

Notes

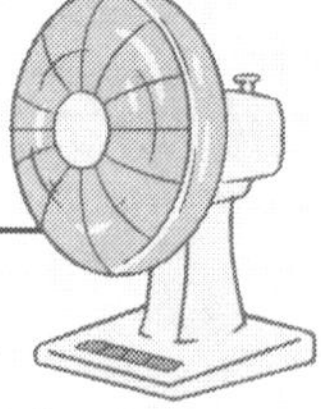

TO DO

Date:

Today's Focus

Priorities List

-
-
-
-
-
-
-
-
-

My Reminder

Notes

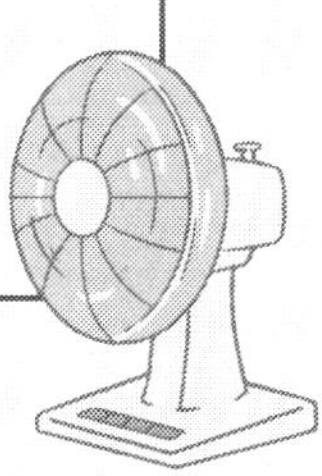

TO DO

Date:

Today's Focus

Priorities List

-
-
-
-
-
-
-
-
-

My Reminder

Notes

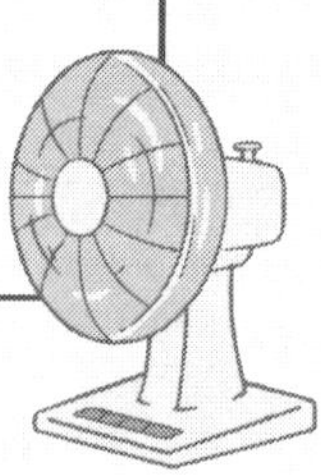

TO DO

Date:

Today's Focus

Priorities List

My Reminder

Notes

TO DO

Date:

Today's Focus

Priorities List

-
-
-
-
-
-
-
-
-

My Reminder

Notes

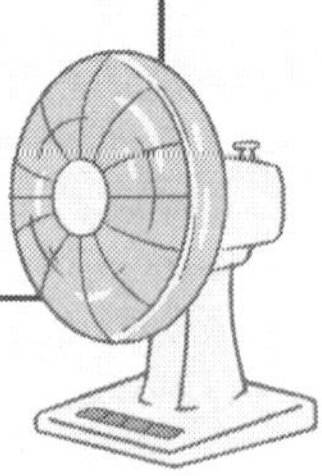

TO DO

Date:

Today's Focus

Priorities List

My Reminder

Notes

TO DO

Date:

Today's Focus

Priorities List

-
-
-
-
-
-
-
-
-

My Reminder

Notes

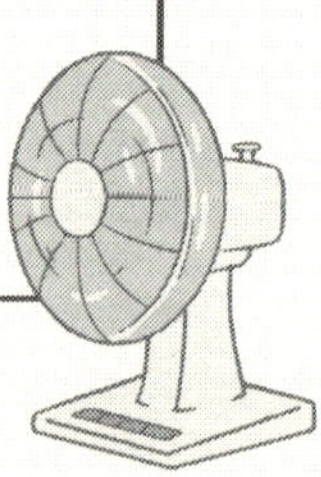

TO DO

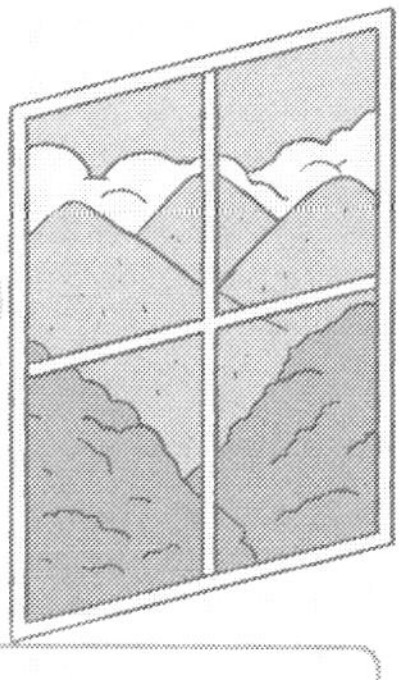

Date:

Today's Focus

Priorities List

My Reminder

Notes

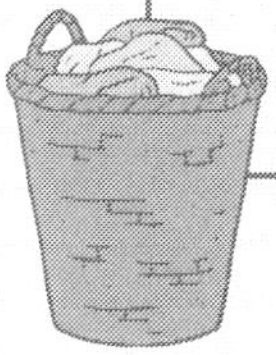

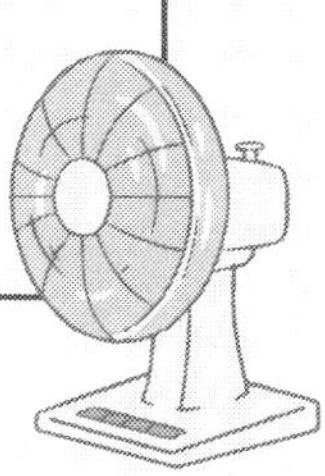

TO DO

Date:

Today's Focus

Priorities List

-
-
-
-
-
-
-
-
-

My Reminder

Notes

TO DO

Date:

Today's Focus

Priorities List

My Reminder

Notes

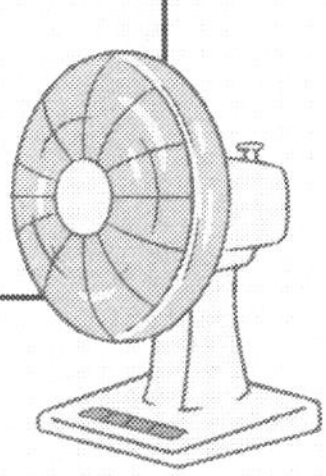

TO DO

Date:

Today's Focus

Priorities List

-
-
-
-
-
-
-
-
-

My Reminder

Notes

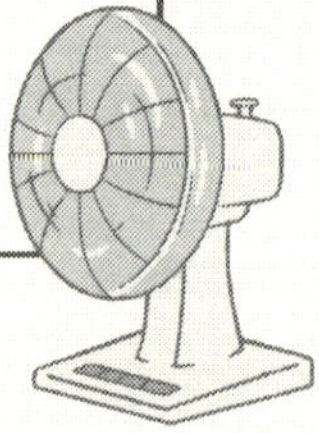

TO DO

Date:

Today's Focus

Priorities List

My Reminder

Notes

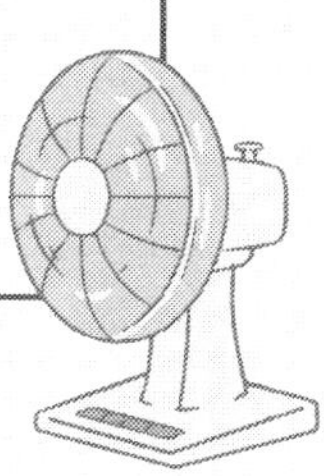

TO DO

Date:

Today's Focus

Priorities List

-
-
-
-
-
-
-
-
-

My Reminder

Notes

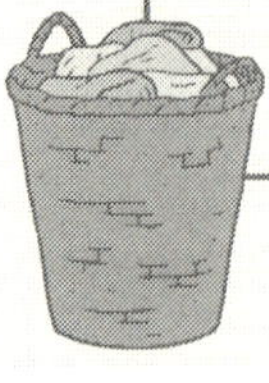

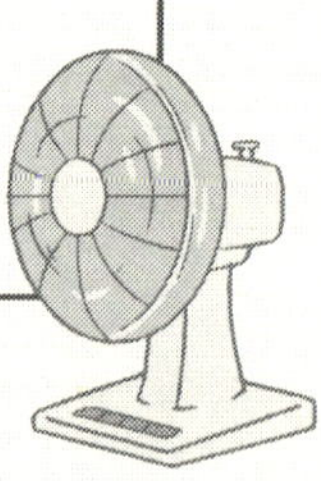

TO DO

Date:

Today's Focus

Priorities List

My Reminder

Notes

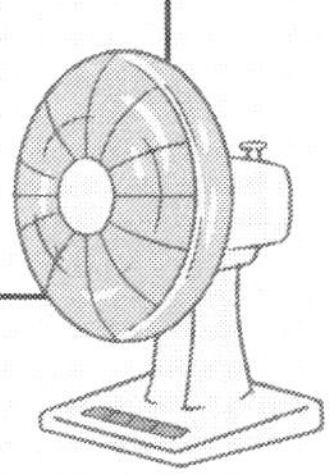

TO DO

Date:

Today's Focus

Priorities List

-
-
-
-
-
-
-
-
-

My Reminder

Notes

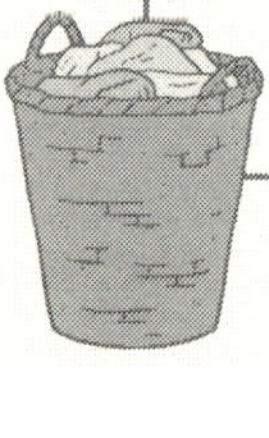

TO DO

Date:

Today's Focus

Priorities List

My Reminder

Notes

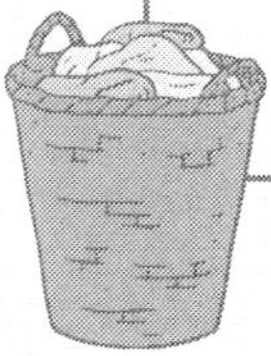

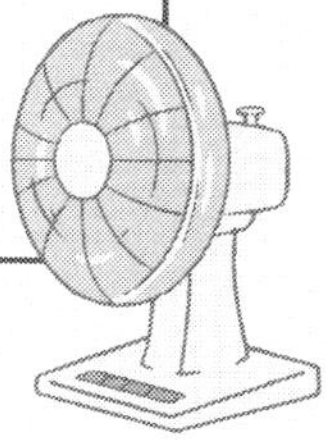

TO DO

Date:

Today's Focus

Priorities List

-
-
-
-
-
-
-
-
-

My Reminder

Notes

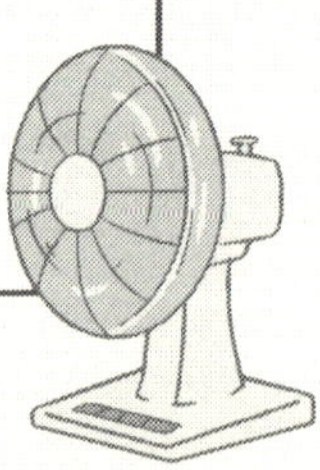

TO DO

Date:

Today's Focus

Priorities List

-
-
-
-
-
-
-
-
-

My Reminder

Notes

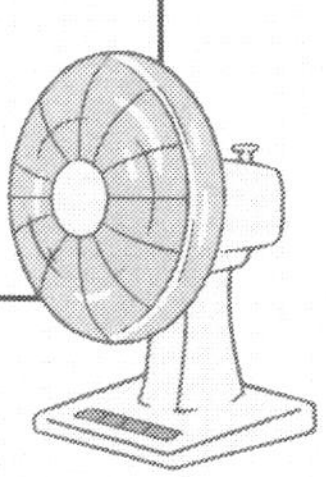

TO DO

Date:

Today's Focus

Priorities List

My Reminder

Notes

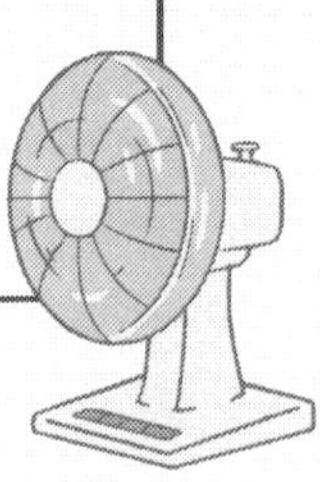

TO DO

Date:

Today's Focus

Priorities List

-
-
-
-
-
-
-
-
-

My Reminder

Notes

TO DO

Date:

Today's Focus

Priorities List

-
-
-
-
-
-
-
-
-

My Reminder

Notes

TO DO

Date:

Today's Focus

Priorities List

-
-
-
-
-
-
-
-
-

My Reminder

Notes

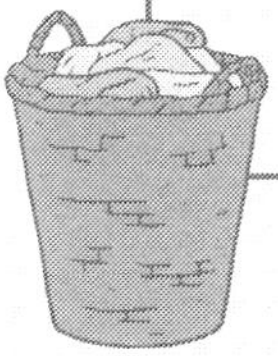

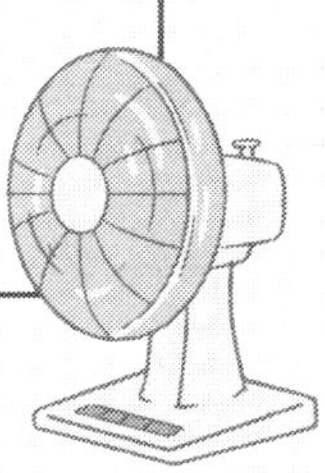

TO DO

Date:

Today's Focus

Priorities List

-
-
-
-
-
-
-
-
-

My Reminder

Notes

TO DO

Date:

Today's Focus

Priorities List

-
-
-
-
-
-
-
-
-

My Reminder

Notes

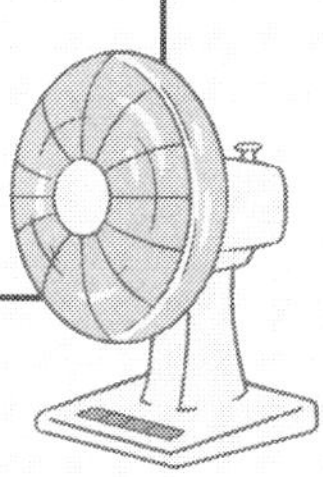

TO DO

Date:

Today's Focus

Priorities List

My Reminder

Notes

TO DO

Date:

Today's Focus

Priorities List

-
-
-
-
-
-
-
-
-

My Reminder

Notes

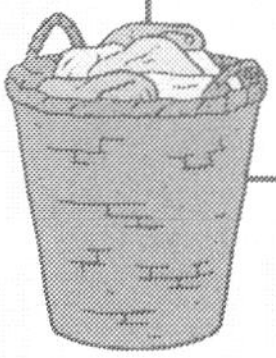

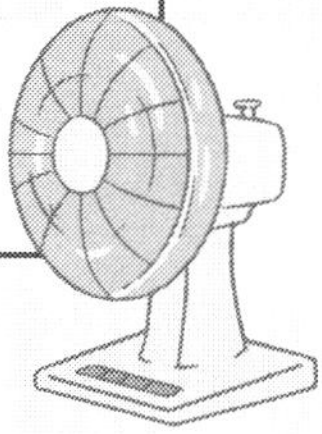

TO DO

Date:

Today's Focus

Priorities List

-
-
-
-
-
-
-
-
-

My Reminder

Notes

TO DO

Date:

Today's Focus

Priorities List

-
-
-
-
-
-
-
-
-

My Reminder

Notes

TO DO

Date:

Today's Focus

Priorities List

-
-
-
-
-
-
-
-
-

My Reminder

Notes

TO DO

Date:

Today's Focus

Priorities List

My Reminder

Notes

TO DO

Date:

Today's Focus

Priorities List

-
-
-
-
-
-
-
-
-

My Reminder

Notes

TO DO

Date:

Today's Focus

Priorities List

-
-
-
-
-
-
-
-
-

My Reminder

Notes

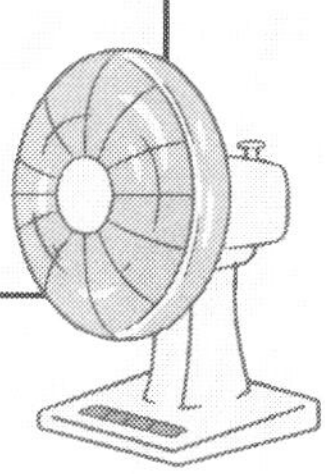

TO DO

Date:

Today's Focus

Priorities List

-
-
-
-
-
-
-
-
-

My Reminder

Notes

TO DO

Date:

Today's Focus

Priorities List

-
-
-
-
-
-
-
-
-

My Reminder

Notes

TO DO

Date:

Today's Focus

Priorities List

My Reminder

Notes

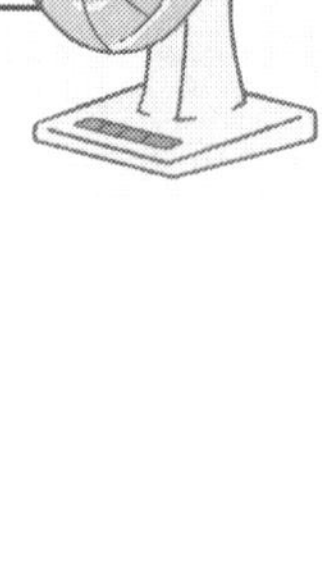

TO DO

Date:

Today's Focus

Priorities List

-
-
-
-
-
-
-
-
-

My Reminder

Notes

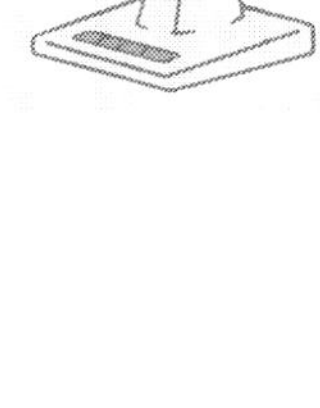

TO DO

Date:

Today's Focus

Priorities List

-
-
-
-
-
-
-
-
-

My Reminder

Notes

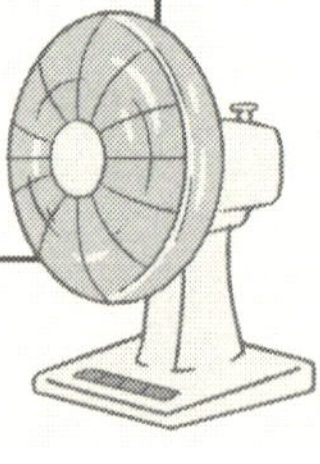

TO DO

Date:

Today's Focus

Priorities List

My Reminder

Notes

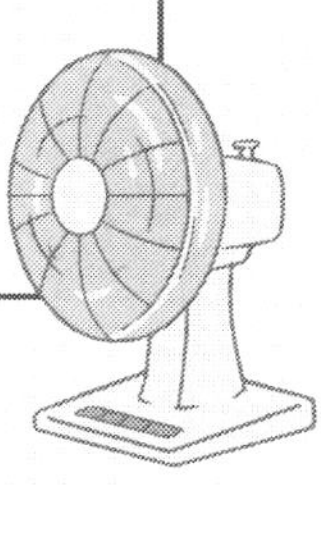

TO DO

Date:

Today's Focus

Priorities List

My Reminder

Notes

TO DO

Date:

Today's Focus

Priorities List

-
-
-
-
-
-
-
-
-

My Reminder

Notes

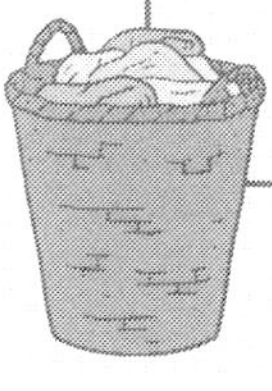

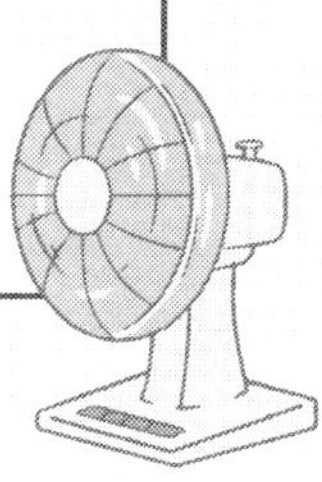

TO DO

Date:

Today's Focus

Priorities List

-
-
-
-
-
-
-
-
-

My Reminder

Notes

TO DO

Date:

Today's Focus

Priorities List

My Reminder

Notes

TO DO

Date:

Today's Focus

Priorities List

-
-
-
-
-
-
-
-
-

My Reminder

Notes

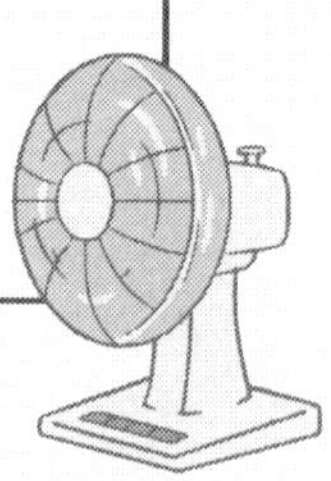

TO DO

Date:

Today's Focus

Priorities List

My Reminder

Notes

Made in United States
Orlando, FL
04 November 2026

90205457R00072